Eva to the Rescue

by Greg Frazier
illustrated by Rick Whipple

Practice Decodable 66

Mc Graw Hill Education

Bothell, WA • Chicago, IL • Columbus, OH • New York, NY

MHEonline.com

Send all inquiries to:
McGraw-Hill Education
8787 Orion Place
Columbus, OH 43240

ISBN: 978-0-02-143433-6
MHID: 0-02-143433-6

Printed in China.

8 9 10 11 12 DSS 27 26 25 24 23

A helicopter was loaded with fuel. Eva, the pilot, got a call.

Kittens were stuck in a river.

"We will go quickly!" she said.

Can Eva rescue them?

Eva looked left and right. She continued to search. Did she see the kittens? Yes!

Eva started the rescue. She lowered the helicopter. Then, Dan helped Trisha get down.

Trisha was next to the kittens. Six kittens mewed sadly. Trisha set them in a basket.

Six kittens were safe! They were lucky. Few kittens get rescued this way.